DINOSAURS

ANKYLOSAURUS

BY GOLRIZ GOLKAR

Kids Core

An Imprint of Abdo Publishing
abdobooks.com

abdobooks.com

Published by Abdo Publishing, a division of ABDO, PO Box 398166, Minneapolis, Minnesota 55439.

Printed in the United States of America, North Mankato, Minnesota.
052025
092025

Cover Photo: Shutterstock Images
Interior Photos: Alberto Andrei Rosu/Shutterstock Images, 4–5; iStockphoto, 6, 12–13, 16, 18; Shutterstock Images, 8, 10 (ankylosaurus), 15, 17, 28–29; Alexandre Laprise/Shutterstock Images, 9; Red Line Editorial, 10 (timeline), 22; Akkharat Jarusilawong/Shutterstock Images, 20–21; DBH1/Alamy, 23; Francois Gohier/Science Source, 24; Universal Studios/Album/Alamy, 26

Editor: Kari Cornell
Series Designer: Mary Shaw

Library of Congress Control Number: 2024949033

Publisher's Cataloging-in-Publication Data

Names: Golkar, Golriz, author.
Title: Ankylosaurus / by Golriz Golkar
Description: Minneapolis, Minnesota: Abdo Publishing, 2026 | Series: Dinosaurs | Includes online resources and index.
Identifiers: ISBN 9781098297312 (lib. bdg.) | ISBN 9798384919834 (ebook)
Subjects: LCSH: Ankylosaurus--Juvenile literature. | Dinosaurs--Juvenile literature. | Herbivores--Juvenile literature. | Paleontology--Juvenile literature. | Extinct animals--Juvenile literature.
Classification: DDC 568.19--dc23

CONTENTS

Ankylosaurs ate ferns and other plants. Some scientists believe they may have been able to dig up roots to eat as well.

AN ARMORED DINOSAUR

An *Ankylosaurus* (an-KEYE-loh-SOHR-uhs) walks slowly in a field. It munches on shrubs and fruits near the ground. Suddenly, it hears a branch crack. It looks up. A dark shadow looms above. It's a *Tyrannosaurus rex*!

Ankylosaurus could whip its tail from side to side to defend itself against a *T. rex*. The force of the tail was enough to break bones.

The giant dinosaur roars. It towers over the short *Ankylosaurus*.

But the *Ankylosaurus* is ready to fight. It swings its strong clubbed tail from side to side.

The *T. rex* steps back. It tries to take a bite. But the bite hurts its jaw. The *Ankylosaurus* is covered with hard armored plates. The *T. rex* cannot bite through them. The giant dinosaur gives up and runs away. The *Ankylosaurus* has won. It fought off a fierce **predator**.

The Extinction of Dinosaurs

Many scientists think that a big rock called an asteroid struck the planet about 66 million years ago. Dust from the asteroid blocked sunlight. Many plants could not grow, so animals died as well. Seventy-five percent of the animals on Earth died. This included the dinosaurs.

Scientists believe that, like other dinosaurs, *Ankylosaurus* reproduced by laying eggs.

The Time of the Dinosaurs

Dinosaurs lived during a time called the Mesozoic Era. This was between 252 million and 66 million years ago. Earth had one

Ankylosaurus footprints are a permanent feature at Torotoro National Park in Bolivia.

large landmass at that time. Earthquakes and volcanic eruptions slowly broke the land into smaller **continents**.

The climate changed over time. Food sources changed too. The dinosaurs adapted. They **evolved** into different **species**.

The Cretaceous period was the last time period of the Mesozoic Era. It lasted from about 145.5 million to 66 million years ago.

The Mesozoic Era

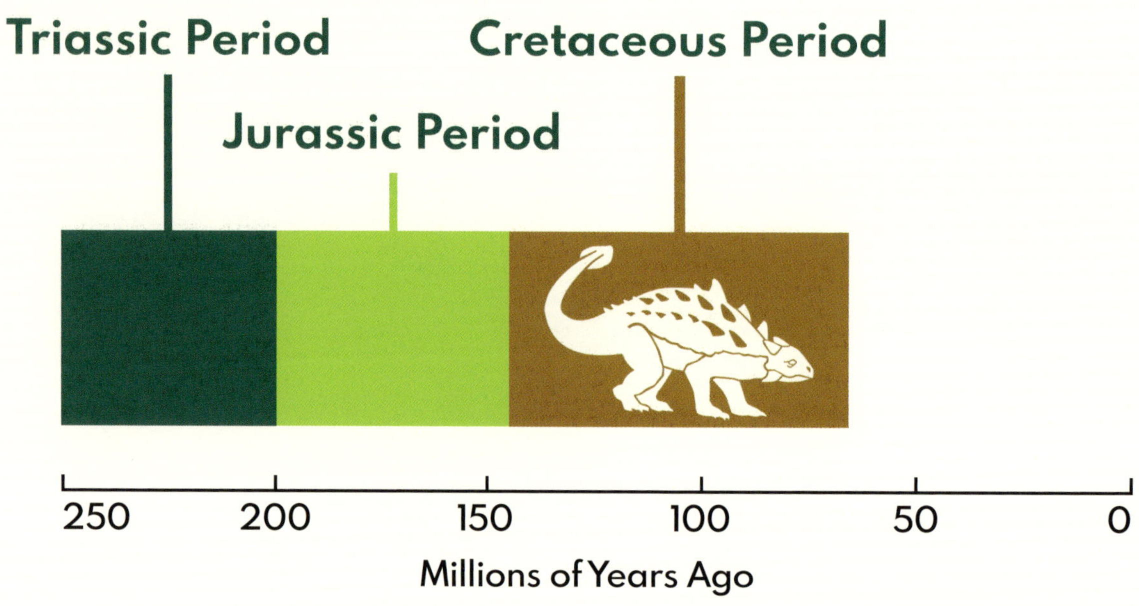

Mammals, dinosaurs, flowering plants, and birds lived during the Mesozoic Era. This was also when dinosaurs became extinct.

During this time, a group of dinosaurs called ankylosaurs emerged. They were four legged and spiky. They roamed the grassy plains of the western United States and parts of Canada.

They also lived in parts of Asia, South America, and Australia.

Ankylosaurs had two main groups. Nodosaurids had narrow heads. Ankylosaurids had wide heads and clubbed tails. Both of these groups were related to stegosaurs. They were also armored dinosaurs. During the late Cretaceous period, one of the ankylosaurs evolved into *Ankylosaurus*.

Explore Online

Visit the website below. Does it give any new information that wasn't in Chapter One?

Cretaceous Period

abdocorelibrary.com/ankylosaurus

In addition to armored plates, *Ankylosaurus* had a row of spikes along the side of its body.

SMALL BUT MIGHTY

Ankylosaurus was the size of a military tank. It walked on four short, strong legs. This dinosaur weighed close to 9,000 pounds (4,080 kg). It was about 4 feet (1.2 m) tall. Some grew to be as long as 35 feet (10.7 m).

This dinosaur had a flat, square-shaped head with four horns. Near its mouth was a small beak. It may have been used to tear plants. The dinosaur's teeth were leaf shaped. They helped *Ankylosaurus* rip up its food. Its large nostrils gave it a good sense of smell. This helped it find food and sense predators.

Ankylosaurus was an **herbivore**. It fed on shrubs and fruits on or near the ground. Scientists believe that in one day, *Ankylosaurus* ate 132 pounds (60 kg) of plants. That's the same amount of food an elephant eats each day. These dinosaurs likely had a special digestive system. This would have helped them break down lots of plants.

Ankylosaurus used its beak and teeth to grind up ferns and other vegetation, but scientists believe it may have eaten tiny insects as well.

Ankylosaurus lived in habitats that offered plenty of vegetation for food. Lakes, rivers, or swamps were often nearby.

Scaring Off Predators

The word *Ankylosaurus* means "fused lizard" in Greek. This refers to the connected body and skull bones of the dinosaur. The bones formed

The spikes on a life-size *Ankylosaurus* model show how they may have looked.

a tough armor. Scutes, which are tough spikes and plates, covered the bony armor. Even the clubbed tail was armored.

Scute Protection

Stegosaurus and *Nodosaurus* were other dinosaurs with protective scutes. Some modern-day animals have them too. Scutes form turtle shells. Crocodile scutes protect the animal's organs during fights with other crocodiles. The scutes also help crocodiles swim and manage their body temperature.

Ankylosaurus used its beak-like mouth to tear leaves from branches and its tiny, pointed teeth to chew them.

Scientists think *Ankylosaurus* probably could not run fast because of its body shape. It could travel only about 3 miles per hour (4.8 km/h). But its body protected it from the fiercest predators. *Ankylosaurus*'s swinging tail could hurt another dinosaur. The armored body was hard to bite.

Further Evidence

Look at the website below. Does it give new evidence to support Chapter Two?

Natural History Museum: *Ankylosaurus*

abdocorelibrary.com/ankylosaurus

One nearly complete *Ankylosaurus* skeleton is on display at the Shanghai Natural History Museum in Shanghai, China.

CHAPTER 3

DISCOVERING ANKYLOSAURUS

Various ankylosaur fossils have been found in the United States, Canada, Europe, and Australia. Many can be seen in museums around the world. But a complete *Ankylosaurus* skeleton has not yet been found. Bones, armor parts, and teeth have been discovered.

Mesozoic Era: Where *Ankylosaurus* Lived

This map shows what the world looked like during the Mesozoic Era. The shaded continents show where ankylosaur fossils have been found.

Barnum Brown, *left*, and Henry Fairfield Osborn work to uncover dinosaur bones in Como Bluff, Wyoming, in 1897.

The first *Ankylosaurus* fossils were found in 1906 in the Hell Creek Formation in Montana. The **paleontologist** Barnum Brown led an **expedition** there. Expedition members discovered most parts of a whole *Ankylosaurus*. His team found more remains on two later expeditions.

An *Ankylosaurus* skull fossil is on display at the Utah State University Eastern Prehistoric Museum in Price, Utah. Scientists believe the dinosaur's brain was the size of a walnut.

These fossils are now displayed at the American Museum of Natural History in New York. In 1947, paleontologist Charles M. Sternberg discovered the biggest *Ankylosaurus* skull ever found. This happened during a fossil dig in Alberta, Canada.

In Popular Culture

Ankylosaurus has appeared in movies and on television shows. The popular *Jurassic Park* series features the dinosaur in the third movie.

Famous Paleontologists

Barnum Brown and Charles M. Sternberg discovered many other dinosaur remains. Sternberg also found a rare mummified *Edmontosaurus*. Brown found the very first *Tyrannosaurus rex* fossils. He later found a more complete *T. rex* in Montana. It can be seen at the American Museum of Natural History in Washington, DC.

An *Ankylosaurus* is one of several dinosaurs shown grazing near a river in *Jurassic Park III.*

Children's TV shows such as *Dinosaur Train* and Pinkfong network's *Little Dino School* teach children about the dinosaur's life. This dinosaur is even shown in video games such as *Fossil Fighters. Ankylosaurus* may have been a short dinosaur, but it was a mighty one!

PRIMARY SOURCE

Barnum Brown discussed the *Ankylosaurus* fossils his expedition found:

> The striking features . . . are its sculptured, plated skull; large flat or low-ridged body plates, some of which are united as a shield.

Source: Barnum Brown. "The Ankylosauridae, a New Family of Armored Dinosaurs From the Upper Cretaceous." *American Museum of Natural History*, 1908, digitallibrary.amnh.org. Accessed 3 Oct. 2024.

Comparing Texts

Think about the quote. Does it support the information in this chapter? Or does it give new information? Explain how in a few sentences.

DINO DETAILS

Clubbed tail with scutes to fight off predators

Scutes on head and whole body for protection
Square and flat head with horns for defense
Four short legs

Glossary

continents
the world's seven major landmasses

evolved
changed over time

expedition
a journey taken for a specific purpose

herbivore
an animal that eats plants

paleontologist
a scientist who studies fossils

predator
an animal that hunts other animals

species
a group of similar living things that can produce young with one another

Online Resources

To learn more about *Ankylosaurus* and late-Cretaceous dinosaurs, visit our free resource websites below.

Visit **abdocorelibrary.com** or scan this QR code for free Common Core resources for teachers and students, including vetted activities, multimedia, and booklinks, for deeper subject comprehension.

Visit **abdobooklinks.com** or scan this QR code for free additional online weblinks for further learning. These links are routinely monitored and updated to provide the most current information available.

Learn More

Chinsamy-Turan, Anusuya. *Dinosaurs and Other Prehistoric Life*. DK, 2021.

Giedd, Steph. *Stegosaurus*. Abdo, 2024.

Yang, Yang. *The Secrets of Dinosaurs*. Brown Books, 2021.

Index

About the Author

Golriz Golkar has written more than 100 nonfiction and fiction books for children. She holds a B.A. in American literature and culture from UCLA and an Ed.M. in language and literacy from the Harvard Graduate School of Education. Golriz lives in France with her husband and young daughter.